COVENANT of GRACE

A Cantata for Holy Week or Eastertide

by Joseph M. Martin • Orchestration by Brant Adams

CONTENTS

Harold F
M U

A Division of Shawnee Press,
1107 17th Avenue South • Nashville, TN 37212

Visit Shawnee Press Online at www.shawneepress.com

About the Cover: Rose Window stained glass design courtesy of Emmanuel Studio Inc.,
410 Maple Avenue, Nashville, Tennessee 37210 www.emmanuelstudio.com.

FOREWORD

Our God is faithful.

He stretches His rainbow across the heavens to remind us of His mercy
and His grace.
He sends streams in the desert and spreads a banquet in the wilderness
providing for the needs of His people.
God loves us with an everlasting love and His faithfulness endures to
every generation.

It was God's perfect love that sent Jesus into the world. All of God's
wondrous promises are made "Yes" in Christ Jesus. The Word became
flesh and dwelt among us...a living promise of truth and light.

As together we take this journey of promises, may your hope be
renewed.
As we recall his life and ministry, may your joy be restored.
As we trace his path to the cross, may your faith be reborn.
As we gaze beyond the shadows of Calvary, may the light of a new
dawn refresh your spirits with peace.

And so we sing waiting for the glorious appearing of our great God and
Savior, Jesus Christ who gave Himself to redeem us and to purify for
Himself a people that are His very own.

This is the covenant of grace.

JOSEPH M. MARTIN

PERFORMANCE NOTES

Each movement of "Covenant of Grace" is intended to celebrate the promises and covenants of God. Through the use of narrators and music, the story of redemption is told.

Some directors may wish to incorporate additional, non-musical elements in their presentation to enhance its meaning. Consider displaying the various names of God, either on banners or in the worship program, to correspond with the central theme of each anthem in the cantata. Here is a list of suggested divine names for each of the movements of the work.

MOVEMENT	NAMES OF GOD
Paean of Promise	JEHOVAH *(the covenant name of God)*
Covenant of the Lamb	JEHOVAH-JIREH *(the Lord will provide)*
For God So Loved the World	IMMANUEL *(God with us)*
Hosanna, Loud Hosanna	KING OF KINGS
The Promise of the Kingdom	MESSIAH *(the Anointed One)*
An Invitation to Grace	JESUS *(God will save)*
Cry of The Crucifixion	MAN OF SORROWS
Here is Love	THE LAMB OF GOD
We Are God's People	CHRIST, THE BRIDEGROOM

Also, feel free to explore other creative options that may help deliver the message of "Covenant of Grace" to the hearts of your people.

It is recommended that, if this work is presented on Easter, an appropriate resurrection hymn be sung to conclude the service.

(The following scripture readings may be placed in the worship bulletin or projected on screens before the "Covenant of Grace" begins. They may also be read following an opening prayer.)

Come unto Me. Listen, so that you may live. I will make with you an everlasting covenant. *(from Isaiah 55)*

"The time is coming," declares the Lord, "when I will make a new covenant. It will not be like the covenant I made with Moses, Abraham and your forefathers."

"This is the covenant I will make," declares the Lord. "I will put my laws in their minds and write them on their hearts. I will be their God, and they will be my people." *(from Hebrews 8)*

Banner:
JEHOVAH *(the covenant name of God)*

in honor of 100 years of music at Trinity Lutheran Church,
Loveland, Colorado, 1905-2005

PAEAN OF PROMISE *

Words and music by
JOSEPH M. MARTIN (BMI)

Lis-ten, faith-ful ser-vant, take cour-age in these words.___ Take

* This octavo, which includes the part for Flute (or C-Instrument), is available separately – A8541.

Grace will for - ev - er en - dure.

Moderately, with expression (♩ = ca. 92)
FLUTE *(or C-Instrument)*

7

A8820

Oh, I will make in you a might - y na - tion,

and I will show - er you with glo - ry from on high._____

Oh, I will bless you, that you might be a bless - ing. This is my prom - ise.

This is my cov - e - nant. This is my

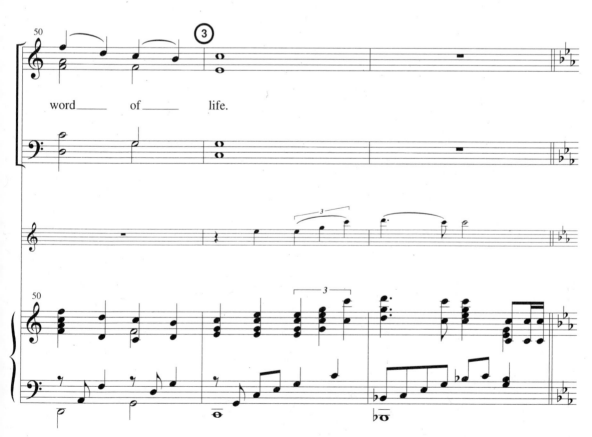

word___ of___ life.

I will bless your night with shin-ing stars of peace and hope.

Ev-'ry val - ley that you walk, you'll nev - er walk a -

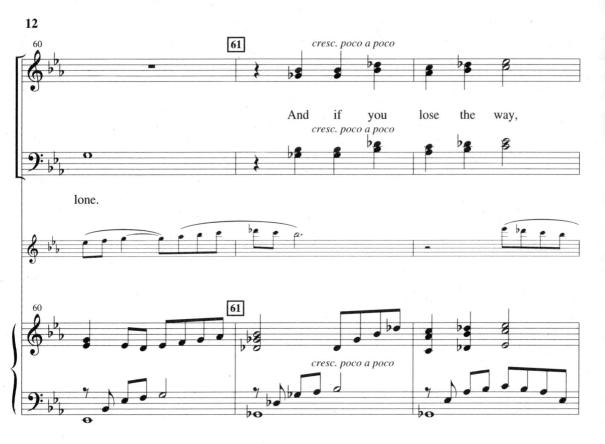

And if you lose the way,

lone.

I'll bring you home a - gain, for you are

cov - ered by my grace.

Oh, I will make of you a might - y

na - tion. Yes, I will show - er you with

bless - ings from on high._____ Oh, I will

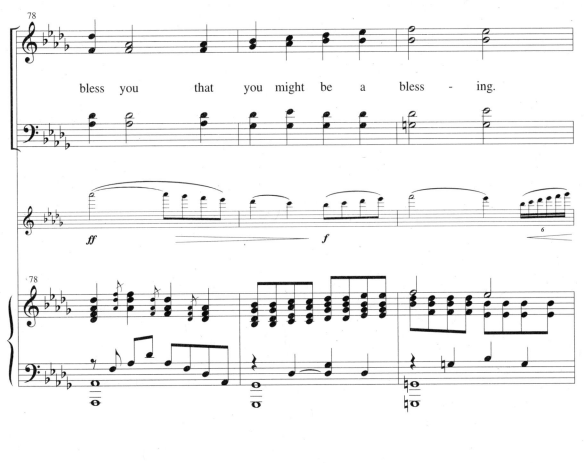

bless you that you might be a bless - ing.

This is my prom - ise. This is my

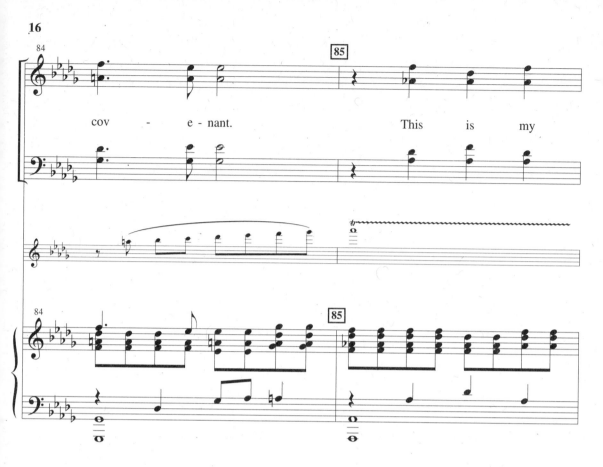

cov - e - nant. This is my

word_____ of _____ life!

This is my cov - e - nant,

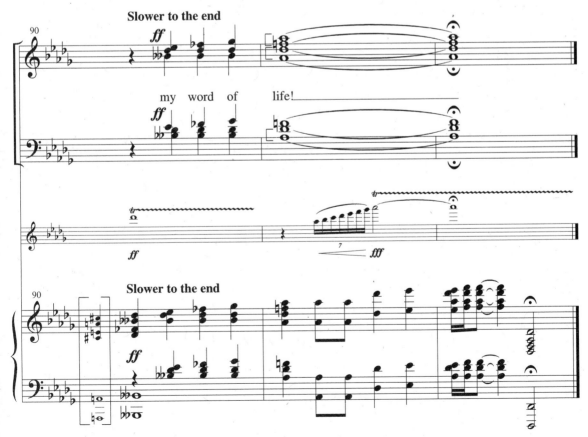

Slower to the end

my word of life!

NARRATOR 1:
Unto Abraham the father of our faith, God made a promise. Abraham would be the patriarch of a great nation. From his lineage would come a chosen people that would lead the world from the wilderness of sin into the promised land of God's amazing grace. God tested Abraham and used his devotion to assure the world that one day, a Redeemer would come.

Listen to the word of the Lord.

NARRATOR 2:
And God said, "Abraham!"

"Here I am," Abraham replied.

"Take your son… your only son, Isaac, whom you love, and go to Moriah and sacrifice him there as a burnt offering upon the mountain."

…So Abraham took the wood for the offering and placed it upon his son, Isaac, and he himself carried the fire and the knife. As the two of them continued on, Isaac spoke up and said, "Father?"

"Yes, my son?" Abraham replied.

"The fire and the wood are here, but where is the lamb?"

Abraham answered, "God Himself will provide the lamb, my son."

And the two of them walked on together. *(from Genesis 22)*

Banner:
JEHOVAH-JIREH *(the Lord will provide)*

commissioned by the Susan Patricia Hodge Foundation,
celebrating the 100th Anniversary, 1908-2008,
Gramling United Methodist Church, Gramling, South Carolina

COVENANT OF THE LAMB

Words by
THOMAS OLIVERS (1725-1799), *alt.*
with additional words by
JOSEPH M. MARTIN (BMI)

Tune: **LEONI**
Traditional Hebrew Melody
and **FOLLOWERS OF THE LAMB**
Traditional Shaker Melody
Arranged by and new music by
JOSEPH M. MARTIN (BMI)

* Tune: LEONI, Traditional Hebrew Melody
Words: Thomas Oliver, 1725-1799, alt.

A8820

bove, the An-cient of E - ter - nal Days and God of

love! Je - ho - vah, great I AM! by

earth and heav'n con - fessed, I bow and bless Thy

heav - en as - cend._____

God is our dwell - ing

place._____ His__ grace__ our__ hearts re -

store. God's mer-cy and His

truth will stand for - ev - er - more!

Joyfully, in two (♩. = ca. 76)

Sing on,___ dance on, cit - i - zens of the prom - ised land.

Sing and re - joice for the cov - e - nant of the Lamb.

joice, re-joice, ho - san - na! Sing ju - bi - lant songs___ and

clap your hands! Re - joice, for God has giv - en the

cov - e - nant of the Lamb! Al - le - lu -

32

A8820

NARRATOR 1:

Unto David, the great King of Israel, God made a promise. Through David's lineage God would bring forth His chosen Messiah. This great King would rule a kingdom of truth and light that would never pass away. He would fulfil the law of Moses. He would build the temple of God deep in the souls of His people and write His word of hope upon their very hearts.

Listen to the word of the Lord.

NARRATOR 2:

The Lord declared unto David, "I will establish a house for you. I will raise up a son from your line and establish His kingdom. He is the one who will build a house for my name and His kingdom will be forever. I will be His Father and He will be my Son." *(from 2 Samuel 7)*

NARRATOR 1:

God's covenant with Abraham and David was fulfilled when the Word became flesh and Jesus was born into the world. God did not spare His only Son, but gave Him up for us all.

The covenant of the law was given through Moses and the prophets, but grace and truth came through Jesus Christ…and there is nothing that can separate us from the love that is in Christ Jesus, our Lord. *(Romans 8:39)*

Banner:
IMMANUEL *(God with us)*

This anthem is dedicated by a grateful congregation in honor of Larry Wolf,
Music Director at Big Beaver United Methodist Church, Troy, Michigan
on the occasion of his 25th Anniversary of faithful service and Music Ministry for the greater glory of God.

FOR GOD SO LOVED THE WORLD*

Based on
John 3:16

Words and music by
JOSEPH M. MARTIN (BMI)

*Octavo available separately: A7961

A8820

to the world to____ con - demn the world,

but that the world through Him might live, that the world through Him might

live, that the world through Him might live._____

He gave His price-less pearl. For God so loved the world, He

gave His on-ly Son. Love came that none should die.

Christ came, a sac-ri-fice, that who-so-ev-er be-

cresc.

lieth in Him,_____ would have e-

ter - nal life, would have e - ter - nal life.

For God so loved the world, He gave His on - ly Son.

NARRATOR 1:

The assurances of the prophets had long echoed through the hearts of the people. Now at last, a new spirit was sweeping across the land as Jesus approached the great city of Jerusalem. This singular moment contained all the hopes and dreams of the people of Israel. They had waited so long for a deliverer. With great celebration, crowds of cheering people greeted the Lord's arrival into the city. With the waving of palms and the ecstatic shouts of a people ready for liberation, the multitudes began to praise God.

NARRATOR 2:

"Hosanna! Hosanna! Blessed is he who comes in the name of the Lord! Blessed is the King of Israel." *(John 12:13)*

Banner:
KING OF KINGS

HOSANNA, LOUD HOSANNA

Words based on
Matthew 21:15-16
by JEANETTE THRELFALL (1821-1880), *alt.*
With additional words by
JOSEPH M. MARTIN

Tune: **ELLACOMBE**
Gesangbuch, Wittenberg, 1784
Arranged by and new music by
JOSEPH M. MARTIN (BMI)

"Ho - san - na, loud ho - san - na," the

breast,   the chil - dren sang their prais - es, the

sim - plest and the best.

Ho-

48

King; O__ may we ev - er praise__ Him__ with

voice,_____

heart and soul and voice, ho - san - na, and

voice,_____

in__ His glo - rious pres - ence, e - ter - nal -ly re -

NARRATOR 1:
In the days following His triumphal entry into Jerusalem, Jesus gathered His disciples close to Him and taught them many things. He opened their eyes and revealed to them the true nature of the kingdom of God.

NARRATOR 2:
"Be prepared…keep your lamps filled with oil and burning bright, for no one knows when the bridegroom shall come for His beloved."
(from Matthew 25)

NARRATOR 1:
He shared with them how in the days ahead, He would suffer to fulfill the law, and to become the author of God's new covenant.

NARRATOR 2:
"In a few days is the Passover, and the Son of Man will be handed over to be crucified." *(Matthew 26:2)*

NARRATOR 1:
All of the promises given to the ancients were now coming true… fulfilled in the one called Jesus.

Banner:
MESSIAH *(the Anointed One)*

for Clif Harris, Minister of Music, Winter Park Baptist Church, Wilmington, North Carolina,
in grateful appreciation of his dedication to the cause of Christ and for 15 years of selfless service to this church

THE PROMISE OF THE KINGDOM

Words by
JOSEPH M. MARTIN
Based on
Matthew 25:31-40

Music by
JOSEPH M. MARTIN (BMI)

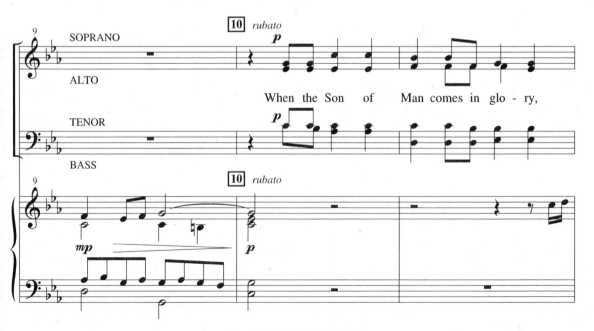

A8820

Come, all who are blessed of my Fa - ther, for yours is the king - dom. Come, ye peo - ple blessed of my Fa - ther, yours is the king - dom, yours is the king - dom of light.

I was a strang-er and you took Me in.

I need-ed clothes and you clothed Me.

When I was sick, you looked aft - er Me.

When I was in pris - on, you came to Me. You

came un - to Me.

yours is the king - dom, yours is the king - dom of God!

Yours is the king - dom,

yours is the king - dom of God!

poco rit. al fine

NARRATOR 1:
On the first day of the Feast of Unleavened Bread, the disciples did as Jesus directed them and prepared the Passover meal. While they were eating, Jesus took bread, gave thanks and broke it, and gave it to His disciples, saying, "Take and eat, this is my body."

NARRATOR 2:
Then Jesus took the cup, gave thanks and offered it to them, saying, "Drink from it, all of you. This is my blood of the covenant, which is poured out for many for the forgiveness of sins. I tell you, I will not drink of this fruit of the vine from now on until that day when I drink it anew with you in my Father's kingdom." *(from Matthew 26)*

Banner:
JESUS *(God will save)*

AN INVITATION TO GRACE

Words and music by
JOSEPH M. MARTIN (BMI)

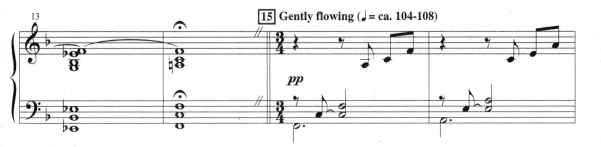

A8820

Come to the table. Here is re-fresh-ment for

seek-ers of life._____ Come, come.

Come to the table. This is the__ cov-e-nant, the__

This is the cov-e-nant, the cov-e-nant _____ of

grace. _____

This is the cov-e-nant of

grace.

NARRATOR 1:

There were many among the religious leaders of the day who did not accept that Jesus was the chosen Messiah. His radical teachings threatened the power and influence they held over the people. Their rigid adherence to the laws of Moses had become an empty ritual, and their hardened hearts knew little of the grace and love that this young Rabbi taught to His followers. Outraged, they secretly conspired to destroy this new movement and its charismatic leader. Betrayed by one of His disciples, Jesus was arrested and brought before members of the Sanhedrin. During His interrogation, the high priest said to Him, "I charge you under oath by the living God: tell us if You are the Christ, the Son of God."

"Yes, it is as you say," Jesus replied.

NARRATOR 2:

Then the high priest tore his clothes and said, "He has spoken blasphemy! Why do we need any more witnesses? Look, now you have heard the blasphemy with your own ears. What shall we do with Him?" *(from Matthew 26)*

"He is worthy of death," they answered.

They spit in His face and struck Him with their fists. Then they handed Him over to a Roman governor named Pontius Pilate. Unwilling to go against the angry mob he allowed Jesus to be taken to Golgotha, where He was crucified. *(from Matthew 27)*

Banner:
MAN OF SORROWS

CRY OF THE CRUCIFIXION!

Tune: **EBENEZER**
by THOMAS J. WILLIAMS (1869-1944)
Arranged by
JOSEPH M. MARTIN (BMI)

Words by
JOSEPH M. MARTIN

King of _____ thorns, re - ceive Your _____ glo - ry!

Come and claim Your cru - el crown.

Prince of tears, Your throne a - waits You,

high a - bove Gol - go - tha's frown.

Now the_____ sol - diers bow be - fore_____ You

as they_____ shout_____ and mock_____ Your name.

Cru - ci - fy the one called___ Je - sus!

Set an - oth - er pris - 'ner free!

We shall___ have no King but___ Cae - sar!

Up Gol - go - tha's

path of ____ mourn - ing, walks the ____ beat - en

Son of _____ Man, to the _____ al - tar, to the _____ slaugh - ter. Come be - hold the dy - ing Lamb. See the _____ cross rise

UNDERSCORE

Based on tune:
WONDROUS LOVE
William Walker's *Southern Harmony*
Arranged by
JOSEPH M. MARTIN (BMI)

NARRATOR: It was there on a desolate windswept hill that Jesus gave His life for the sins of the world. Lifted high on a cross of shame, Jesus became a sacrifice and reconciled us to himself. The ancient promise made to Abraham had been kept... God had provided a Lamb.

His arms

outstretched, Jesus embraced the world with forgiveness and a new covenant of grace was

accomplished.   "It is finished," He cried and across the vastness of time

the echoes of a distant promise rang out,   "See I have loved you with

an everlasting love; I have drawn you close and covered you with loving-kindness and unfailing
grace. Do not be afraid. Do not be discouraged. I will never leave you or forsake you...

I will never forget you. Look...I have engraved you in the palms of my hands.

Banner:
THE LAMB OF GOD

commissioned by the Springhill United Methodist Church Chancel Choir, Springhill, Louisiana,
in honor of Dr. Gene Wilson Kelsay, Minister of Music for 32 years

HERE IS LOVE

Words by
WILLIAM REES (1802-1883) *alt.*

Tune:
DYMA GARIAD
by ROBERT LOWRY (1826-1899)
Arranged by
JOSEPH M. MARTIN (BMI)

Prince of Life, our ran-som,____ shed for us His pre - cious

blood. Who His love will not re - mem-ber?____ Who can

TENOR

BASS

cease to sing His praise? He can nev - er be for-

got-ten___ through-out heav'n's e - ter - nal days.

On the

mount of cru - ci - fix - ion,___ foun-tains o - pened, deep and

wide._____ Through the flood - gates of God's mer - cy_____ flowed a

vast and grac - ious tide. Grace and love, like might - y

riv - ers, poured in - ces - sant___ from a - bove,_____ and God's

peace____ and per-fect jus-tice____ kissed a guilt - y world in

love.____ Grace and love, like might-y

riv-ers,____ poured in - ces - sant from a - bove, and God's

peace and per-fect jus-tice___ kissed a guilt - y world in

love.

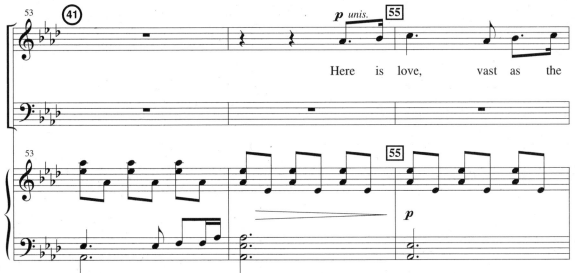

Here is love, vast as the

o - cean.＿＿＿＿＿＿ Here is

Here is love, vast as the o - cean.＿

love. Here is love.＿

Here is love.＿

NARRATOR 1: *(reading slowly)*
Set me as a seal upon your heart, as a seal upon your right arm. Many waters cannot quench love, neither can the floods drown it, for love is stronger than death…love is stronger then death…love is stronger than death. *(Song of Solomon 8:6)*

(If performed during Holy Week you may consider ending the work here. The quiet simple singing or playing of "My Jesus, I Love Thee," can be an effective benediction and the service can end in the spirit of contemplation. If a more celebrative conclusion is desired, then sing the anthem, "We Are God's People." This anthem celebrates the final covenant between Christ, the Bridegroom, and His bride, the church triumphant.)

Banner:
CHRIST, THE BRIDEGROOM

commissioned by the Chancel Choir of Friendswood United Methodist Church
for the consecration of their new Worship Center at Friendswood, Texas, October 21, 2007,
and with deep appreciation to Rev. Terry L. Bebermeyer, Minister of Music,
for his guiding spirit and many years as a faithful and dedicated servant

WE ARE GOD'S PEOPLE

Words by
JOSEPH M. MARTIN
and J. PAUL WILLIAMS (ASCAP)

Music by
JOSEPH M. MARTIN (BMI)

* Tune: AURELIA, Samuel S. Wesley, 1810-1876
  Words: Samuel J. Stone, 1839-1900

A8820

be His ho - ly bride. With

His own blood He bought her and for her life He died.

(Optional)
NARRATOR: Let us rejoice and be glad and give Him glory! For our Lord God Almighty reigns.

With steady confidence (♩ = ca. 69)

"Blessed are those who are invited to the wedding feast of the Lamb!"

bride of Christ, re - deemed for - ev - er - more.

We are God's peo - ple. We are the cho - sen of our

Lord.

dim. poco a poco

read-y. Our lamps are bright.

Our lamps are burn-ing bright. Your church is

We are wait-ing to be your ho-ly bride.

wait-ing to be your ho-ly bride.

cresc.

Lord, make us wor-thy. Lord, wash our

gar - ments in Your light.

We are God's peo - ple. We are the

chil - dren of grace.   We are God's peo - ple.

We are one   in   love's em-brace._____

We   are   the   bride   of   Christ, re - deemed for - ev - er -

Lord!

We are the peo - ple of

God!